# got a minute?

## reflections in faith

by:

Greg Wasinski

got a minute?


Cover Design by Frank J. Wasinski III



Printed in the United States of America

ISBN: 978-0-9860269-3-5

**Learn more at:**
**www.GregWasinski.com**

# Dedication

For Nathan and Natalie

In a world of noise, distractions, and confusion –
I pray you will always find at least one minute each day
to reflect on how much God loves you and I adore you.

# Table of Contents

# Introduction

---

*"For I know the plans I have for you," declares the Lord, "plans to prosper you and not to harm you, plans to give you hope and a future." (Jer 29:11)*

---

We live busy lives. Worse yet, we allow so many distractions to steal so much of the time we do. Too often God takes a back seat to the things of this world that we feel *must* get done. However, I have learned that if we give Him a portion of our time each day, with our whole heart, not only do we find ourselves more inspired to get things done, but we also allow God to be at the center of everything we do.

This devotional is not meant to overwhelm you. It is specifically set up as a weekly reflection so each day, for seven days, we can work together on *ONE* principle. I love daily devotionals, but sometimes it seems like a great lesson is lost twenty-four hours after we read it. We move on to perfect another aspect of our life before we fully grasp the message placed on our heart.

The "journal" pages have seven different areas where you should write your own reflection every day of the week. Each day is a new opportunity to re-read the chapter and concentrate on how the message speaks to you that day; things can be very different.

*got a minute?* gives us direction. A guide to illuminate the path we need to take, putting aside our own pride to grow closer to God with a relationship that goes deeper than we normally allow it. Our role for His Kingdom is not just to be merely a Sunday participant of worship, but to be an every-day disciple striving to live a

holy life for ourselves, our families, our friends, our communities, and ultimately for the One who created us. A living example of what it means to be a believer in Jesus Christ. Even more so, an active witness who puts your faith on display without saying a word.

This set of reflections is meant to be a supplement to other ways you encounter our Lord - ***never a substitute for Scripture, church attendance, or other foundational learning***. My prayer is that you too can find relation to each theme in your own unique way. Allowing God into places of your heart you have kept Him from before or possibly gain the courage you need to invite others to join you on your journey. We know God deserves way more than one minute of our time each day, but if we begin each day by offering just sixty seconds to Him, we will find that He slowly will become part of all we do. Pray for me and I'll pray for you.

Peace,

***PS: Take this journal with you to Mass or Sunday worship and reflect on your weekly journey. Take notes during the service and what you might be hearing as a reminder God is always speaking to you.***

---

*What is your hope that this devotional can help you with and how can you be transformed over the next year? Declare it on the next page and write some goals.*

---

# DECLARATION

# A Note About the Gifts of the Spirit

*"The Holy Spirit is given to each of us in a special way. That is for the good of all." (1Cor 12:7)*

One thing that's important for us to understand, and I really can never repeat it enough is that, you are never alone in your journey. The Holy Spirit guides you and fulfills you in the unseen.

Throughout *got a minute?* I have highlighted a different gift of the Holy Spirit that Catholic Christians are sealed with during the Sacrament of Confirmation. You actually receive these gifts at Baptism, but in your "Yes" to Christ, our senses to utilize these gifts are heightened.

The seven gifts are: *Wisdom, Understanding, Right Judgement, Knowledge, Courage, Reverence, Wonder and Awe*. Every seventh week I explain the real-life application to give these gifts meaning to our lives.

Each one of us is called to live a life of prayer, evangelization and stewardship. Some days we are not exactly sure where to begin, but that's when we must rely on the power of the Holy Spirit and draw strength from the gifts we are given.

Our ability to fall back on these gifts helps us to not only experience things in the world as God wants us to, but to also help us with our own internal reflection process. Continuing to form a strong healthy relationship with the Creator and His Son, Jesus Christ.

# Faith as the Crust

*"Whatever you do, work heartily, as for the Lord and not for men." (Col 3:23)*

Whether it's our work, sports, relationships, or whatever other activities we engage in, we can get caught up in the details of the result rather than building a strong foundation. God must be part of it all.

Imagine your day as a pie chart of all the things that have to get done. If we include God, we would most likely only have a tiny sliver dedicated to prayer. Amidst our tasks, eating, sleeping, etc., we tend to give God just a small piece of our day - usually at the end. What if instead, we allowed Him to be part of it all - the good and the bad? What if we allowed him to be the crust of our "daily pie" calling on Him for support?

On your way to work – pray for strength to allow Christ to lead you. Before you take the field or court in sports – thank God for your talent and ask Him to protect you. When cleaning your home – see God's blessing in the mess while praying for others who don't have a home to clean.

If we can remind ourselves that our faith should be at the base of everything we do, holding it all together, our ability to see God in everything every day comes into complete focus. Allow faith to be your crust, and soon those you love will begin living that way too.

*How can you invite God into all your activities and daily routines? Let Him in and recall what it means each day.*

# JOURNAL

# Seek and Crave

*"Seek the Lord and his strength; seek his presence continually!" (1Chron 16:11)*

There is a difference between *wanting* something and fighting to get what you desire. It isn't enough to make a half-hearted effort toward your goals, you must claw and scratch, kick and scream with all your heart, mind, and body.

The Greek word *Epizeteo* is used fourteen times in the new testament when people are "looking" for signs from God or working to find a relationship with Him. But it doesn't just mean "to search," it means "to *seek*," "to *crave*," letting nothing stop you from finding God.

If you've ever given up something you once loved to do, stopped an addiction, or even started a diet routine, you know that you really crave to experience any nuance of what you gave up. Once you are able to have a treat, you run to your guilty pleasure and nothing will stop you from experiencing it.

Our relationship to find and experience Christ should be the same way. Not just something we "kind of want" but instead a desire to know Him in new ways - and nothing will stop us from having Him close to our side. Maybe it's time for your faith to take on a new level of desiring God in a way you haven't before.

*How can you intentionally seek out Christ daily, other than only when you need something?*

# JOURNAL

# Truth and Love

*"Children, let us love not in word or speech but in deed and truth.." (1Jn 3:18)*

One of the beautiful aspects about Scripture, is the recurrence of certain themes. A particular message throughout the bible is the need to share our faith with both *truth* and *love* - not one without the other.

When we embrace that truth and love exist together our interactions become rooted in both - remembering how we both *give* and *receive* advice. For example, if we are journeying with a friend through a bad situation, we must listen with compassion while offering solutions that are for the greater good of everyone.

Even when making decisions for our self, *truth* and *love* together prevent us from justifying bad choices for selfish reasons. A life of faith isn't always about a "feel good" message that allows us to make excuses for behavior that goes against God's laws.

To deliver something we feel is truth without love is taken as pure criticism. If we offer love without truth, then we are in danger of allowing someone else to head in the opposite direction of God. The only way we lead those we care about to heaven is to make sure we're the image of God's love while being challenged to walk in the light of truth.

*Think about recent conversations, advice you've shared, or been given. Did it offer both truth and love?*

# JOURNAL

# Perfectly Imperfect

*"And I am sure of this, that he who began a good work in you will bring it to completion ..." (Phil 1:6)*

Seeing ourselves through the eyes of God can be difficult for most of us. We forget He made each of us with His own hands. We are unfinished masterpieces continually under construction - perfectly imperfect.

God is like the artist who sees what's inside the concrete block and wants to set it free – He knows our full potential when He is working to reveal His masterpiece. However, even after it's on display for the world to see, it gets bumped around, rubbed the wrong way, even dropped, and it will need some touch ups.

The Creator doesn't see imperfections how we see them. For Him, they're another opportunity to open our hearts to recognize He loves us. Despite the image our mind sees of who we are, or the sinful flaws we have, the Father sees our potential. Sometimes, He takes our scars and highlights them for the realism they display.

God continually takes you into His workshop through personal prayer time, faith formation and Mass. It's all part of the one-on-one time He needs to fill in the cracks and chisel away the portions that aren't supposed to be there, fixing what life has broken. Our lives will remain perfectly imperfect because we're never fully complete until we share eternity with Him.

*What are areas of your life God is desiring to remake or fix? Are you allowing Him to do what He needs?*

# JOURNAL

# Just Pray

*"When you call me, and come and pray to me,*
*I will listen to you." (Jer 29:12)*

Quite often in life, we forget the basics. Especially when tough times roll in, our humanness isn't sure what to do next. In these times emptiness or despair leave us feeling hopeless. If we don't dig in, we will spiral out of control, forgetting the fundamentals to let God be God.

When struggling, our first thought becomes "now what?" The immediate answer is so simple, so easy, yet so difficult at the same time: *just pray*. Open yourself up for the opportunity to share yourself with God and hear what He is saying in return. Even if you cannot think of the right things to say or pray, simply ask God to listen to your heart.

The one important thing that we must accept when we decide to *just pray*, is that the prayers we offer are not for what we want, but what God needs us to be. Our prayers must become ones of patience, clarity, openness, and understanding. Our petitions must be offered with a heart focused on God and ears open to absorb His response. Think of Jesus in the Garden during His deepest moment of despair... He just prayed.

When things don't make sense and reason seems distant, our peace will only be found when we get on our knees for the first time or the millionth to just pray.

*What situations have you been struggling with that you have forgotten to take fully to prayer?*

# JOURNAL

# Effective Habits

*"Solid food is for the mature, because of practice have their senses trained to discern good and evil." (Heb 5:14)*

The world of self-help offers many books and methods to help us grow by forming highly effective habits. Sometimes they're broken out into seven simple steps that don't seem so simple at all to maintain. This happens if the habits we're trying to form aren't grounded in the thing we need to rely on: our faith.

A great motivational speech can excite us, but on its own, it can't sustain us - something is missing. We must be open to routines that invite God into the journey give us the "X Factor" people don't talk about. God makes us strong, organized, determined, and able to excel in whatever area of life we're trying to focus on making better. By including our faith, effective habits become holy habits - not to say they only relate to church, but that God is continually blessing our efforts. Our inspirational resources shouldn't just be about worldly wants, they should consist of holy people who show us how to be "*IN*" the world, not "*OF*" the world.

Intermix spiritual reading along with inspirational resources. Create a calendar reminder on your phone for a quick mid-day prayer. Journal before bed to review your day. Bottom line form effective habits that keep God at the center and you'll accomplish all you desire.

*What faith-based routines can you incorporate in your day to help you form the habits you need most?*

# JOURNAL

# WISDOM

*"Wisdom is more precious than rubies; nothing you desire can compare with her." (Prov 3:15)*

Our first gift of the Holy Spirit we focus on is WISDOM. It's our ability to see things as God sees them. It gives us the openness to praise God in the good and in the bad.

With the gift of WISDOM, we can put our faith into action by continuing to live what we believe, even when we don't understand. This gift gives us the ability to surrender to God's ultimate love for us.

The gifts of the Spirit give us the ability to do things we think are impossible. To deal with things that as humans, don't even make sense. I often think WISDOM was the gift that would have given Joseph the ability to take Mary into his home and follow the will of God as the leader of the Holy Family.

Our world today seems to lack the WISDOM that can provide insight into humanity. It's how we look outside ourselves during the times where evil has perpetrated outward hate and envy. If we experienced things as God does, it would allow us to respond with charity and patience despite our human emotions.

View life with God's eyes by allowing WISDOM to help you live what you believe by finding the light in the dark and even healing while the hurt still exists.

*Spend this week praying for Wisdom to lead your heart. What situations can this gift help with?*

# JOURNAL

# Living a Life of Joy

*"Until now you've asked nothing in my name. Ask, and you will receive, that your joy may be full." (Jn 16:24)*

Most of Jesus' miracles were performed during *everyday* routines of life. They were done for people He simply encountered along the way. Such as the healings of the blind men, the woman bleeding for years, the paralytic, the leper, and even as He carried the cross.

Not only does Jesus want to meet us at church, but also in our day where we don't usually remain open to see Him. Staying vigilant prevents us from becoming complacent in faith, taking certain things for granted, or even getting frustrated by doing everyday tasks that seem like a burden. Every second of life is a chance to encounter Jesus and profound joy.

Living a life of joy consists of taking the ordinary and allowing God to open our eyes to the blessings that exist within any moment. As you work to complete your "chores" or head to your job, find joy in them and allow God to be part of all of it. Allow your everyday routines to turn from a strain on time to a holy moment. By joyfully including the Lord you might even experience a miracle along the path. For example:

- *Cutting Grass – Gratitude for having a yard.*
- *Doing Dishes – Blessing of food you ate.*
- *Work Commute – Pray for those without a job.*
- *(You get the idea... Continue with your own.)*

*Think of your chores, how can you change the way you think about them by including Christ to be with you?*

# JOURNAL

# What they Want

*"Whatever you do, work heartily, as for the Lord and not for men." (Col 3:23)*

Recently, while reading C.S. Lewis, I was reminded that our history's struggles of money, ambition, war, and slavery are all part of man trying to find something other than God in order to be happy.

The Catechism of the Catholic Church, paragraph 27, tells us that every human heart desires happiness by living in unity with the Father who created them, and nothing can be done apart from Him.

No matter what we do on our own, if it doesn't include God in some way, it will never fulfill us. As humans, we long for clarity, inner peace, and prolonged joy – the question is, where are we looking to find it?

So, when I say, *"give them what they want,"* I'm asking you to have the courage to surrender to being God's instrument and trust Him to use you so He can provide others all they truly seek. While they may not exactly know it's what they want, we have to help nurture them through what we know about God to give it to them anyway.

Let's be brave enough to live our faith out loud to inspire others to form the relationship they need to experience the life they want. Then with love and truth, let's help others find what was there all along.

*Who are the people God is calling you to help "get what they truly want" this week?*

# JOURNAL

# The Mountain Top

*"The mountains may depart and the hills removed, but my steadfast love shall not depart from you, and my covenant of peace shall not be removed..." (Is 54:10)*

In our faith, we can make God some prize to be attained. He becomes relegated to experiences or answered prayers that we call mountain top moments. Usually great joy and excitement are felt when at the top. It's why we like Sunday Mass, retreats/renewals and any encounter where we will feel Christ so strongly at our side. We can forget He is with us always.

Faith journeys can be like life. We want to reach our goal so quickly we run to the top of the "mountain" with so much gusto, we can't stop – we slide down the other side without enjoying the apex of our journey.

At the same time, if we do stop and appreciate the view with Him at the top, it isn't realistic that every moment will feel the way it does during a vivid holy moment. We must pause and gain our strength at the top to be ready when we head back down to the bottom to maintain any transformations we experience.

It's okay to stare up and long for the mountain top again but stay aware - life isn't lived on the mountain top. It's about how we prepare for our journey in the valley. Remember what we learn, who we became, and what God revealed during a "Transfiguration" moment.

*Name some "mountain top" moments you've had. What did you learn? Did you pause to appreciate them?*

# JOURNAL

# Hidden Answers

*"He made known to us the mystery of His will, according to His kind intention which He purposed in Him" (Eph 1:9)*

We tend to offer up prayers with a specific result in mind. It might be for a change in a health diagnosis, healing in a relationship or maybe even an end to financial struggles.

Whatever the situation is (or what we're desperate for) God to help us with, we have to remember that once we lift these intentions up to the Lord, we must be willing to keep our eyes open to the hidden answers. Ones that aren't what we expect but instead what we need. Ones that help us in our situation in a way we might not expect.

That prayer for health may not mean a cure but the right people to bring peace and comfort. A cry to repair a relationship could give you the grace to forgive even when it's not your fault. And a request for money could mean getting the right customer service agent who gets you extra time needed for bills until things turn around.

God answers our prayers in many different forms. When we accept this and see things through the lens of faith, hidden answers we hadn't noticed before are revealed.

*Think about recent prayers, are there situations God gave you what you needed in a hidden way?*

# JOURNAL

# The Slow Leak

---

*"How blessed is he who considers the helpless; The LORD will deliver him in a day of trouble." (Psalm 41:1)*

---

I love that we are always looking to help people in the greatest need. We can refer to these people as "broken" or on the "margins." The only problem is that we define *greatest need* through signs that we can see. After all, if someone has a physical appearance of the cross they bear, it's a lot easier for us to notice them.

But day in and day out, there are people around us experiencing what I call *"the slow leak."* Individuals who carry a cross of tremendous weight that no one knows about. While they smile to display strength on the outside, they are dying on the inside. It might be the mental illness of a child, an abusive relationship, job loss, or just a feeling that no one in the world cares.

Just like a tire on our car: If we don't pay attention to the slow leak of air coming from a damaged part, it eventually become flat. Not only can it not continue, sometimes they are damaged beyond repair.

Remember we are called to be the image of Christ for those most in need, but that does not always mean that their desperation will be apparent. Take notice of all people, it could be your awareness that gives hope to the hopeless, saves a marriage, inspires the broken, or even prevents a suicide.

---

*Who can you focus your attention on that needs to be "healed" before they become completely broken?*

---

# JOURNAL

# Claimed by Choice

*"You did not choose me, but I chose you and appointed you that you should go and bear fruit and that your fruit should abide..." (Jn 15:16)*

So often we forget the simple fact that God "claims" us as His own. Not because we choose Him, but because we are part of Him as His child.

Everything about us is unique so we may fulfill the exact purpose for why we have been placed on this Earth. In our faith, we define this as our *vocation*. We don't get to pick our gifts or even the situation we are born into, but God is always nudging us in the direction that best uses our talents.

Remember, the word *vocation* isn't just associated with the ordained religious or priesthood, but includes married, single and those living the consecrated life.

The vocation we are being called into, or we have already been living, falls into accordance with God's ultimate desire for us to be filled with His grace. Fighting our vocation can leave us feeling empty inside.

Find peace in being the person God has claimed you by choice to do great things for His Kingdom. Be open enough to not only discern where He is leading you but take time to reflect on where you have been - in both thoughts you will find your vocation within and the inner peace you desire.

*Are you obediently following God's call for you? Identify the gifts God has blessed you with - are you using them?*

# JOURNAL

# UNDERSTANDING

*"Count it all joy, my brothers, when you meet trials of various kinds, for you know that the testing of your faith produces steadfastness." (James 1:2)*

The Gift of UNDERSTANDING offers us the ability to fully grasp our faith; beginning to understand things as God understands them.

Often, we find ourselves lost in a world that headlines and events are glorified outside the bounds of what we believe. During these moments, we must rely on this gift to fully live the life we are taught in Scriptures and church teaching.

As we lead others to Heaven, UNDERSTANDING allows us to forgive, sympathize and identify with all those who struggle to surrender to a life centered on Jesus Christ. It helps us take a chance on people we normally wouldn't because it is God who ultimately knows their heart and soul. We move beyond their shortcomings to journey with them in some way.

As we live our faith in the real world, we must fully rely on the Spirit's ability to help us see *growth begins where blame ends*. UNDERSTANDING is the key to grasping how we can accept things as God would.

If we have WISDOM to see things with God's eyes, then we must accept UNDERSTANDING as experiencing faith and others with His mind.

*Pray for Understanding with people you are struggling with by name - How can God help you relate to them?*

# JOURNAL

# Mercy

*"'I desire mercy, not sacrifice.' For I have not come to call the righteous, but sinners." (Mt 9:13)*

I was asked the question once, "What is the difference between *forgiveness* and *mercy*?" For the record, this is not an easy or short answer. What came to mind was the Sacramental gift found in Marriage. Because, over the years, there are times couples struggle, for one reason or another, to move beyond the hurts that occur. Deep scars aren't forgiven easily, but mercy is offered with love for the sake of their bond. Even if you aren't married this same level of thinking needs to be applied to friendships, family, and humanity in general.

How many times has the Lord been merciful to you when you've fallen? To fully grasp what it means to be merciful means we must spiritually pardon, the unforgivable with compassion. To be real, extending mercy doesn't mean we can turn off our brain's feelings and forget the hurt. Forgetting the offense might never be possible. After all, the devil uses it to create division.

Make the effort to live in the image of Christ by focusing once again on mercy. Find the strength to offer mercy in a way that saves a marriage, prevents separation of family, or gives dignity to someone in need. Remember, one day it just might be you who needs to seek mercy from another.

*Who needs your mercy? Pray for the strength to be able to offer it and over time forget the pain.*

# JOURNAL

# The Company We Keep

*"Do not be deceived: 'Bad company ruins good morals.'" (1Cor 15:33)*

Have you ever noticed Jesus knew exactly what each person He surrounded Himself with needed? He knew who He could trust, who needed compassion, and who He should challenge. He even knew who would betray Him.

Every day we are surrounded by people who are part of our little world. A circle of friends, family, co-workers, and the occasional stranger who we invest our time in. We influence them and they influence us. We continually are helping each other steer away from bad decisions or possibly be led farther away from Christ.

It is good occasionally to make a list of those closest to us and pray on each relationship. This helps us identify those who don't have our best interest in mind or the "*takers*" who we need to proceed with cautiously. Also, it reminds us that we have a responsibility to other people, recognizing what they might need us to be for them.

Continually analyzing the company we keep opens our eyes to see if they are helping us in our relationship of faith or if we are the ones who need to do a better job of leading them to Christ.

*Make a list of friends and those you are closest to. Identify those you need to guide, those who guide you, and those who are toxic to your life.*

# JOURNAL

# Love Wins

*"And now these three remain: faith, hope and love. But the greatest of these is love." (1Cor13:13)*

Have you ever been in a relationship where something rocks the very foundation it was built on? Quite possibly at first glance the only option is to run away. In the end, you stay because love wins, and the power of love has an amazing influence. If God was willing to give His Son to die because of His love for us, then we can believe it will do amazing things for us.

Anytime we become lost, hurt, or even scared, we begin to question things we know are true. Even our relationship with God and our faith can experience moments when fear causes us to question the love of what we believe. In these times, we must fall back on the one thing God never stops giving us: love.

Love is what we hold on to when all else fails - or as St. Paul told the Corinthians, "Love bears all things, believes all things, hopes all things, endures all things." (1Cor 13:7) This is our reminder that *LOVE ALWAYS WINS*. Love is the most essential thing we can hold on to when our world is falling down around us.

If you ever wonder how you are going to make it through the storm you're in, look at the cross to remember that not only is love enough, it is EVERYTHING.

*Do you admire relationships where love is so evident? How will you pray for love to win where fear exists?*

# JOURNAL

# It's A Long Road

*"In their hearts humans plan their course, but the Lord establishes their steps." (Prov 16:9)*

The unanswered prayer, or even the day where nothing goes right, can put a chink in the armor of our faith. Most often, instead of surrendering it all back to God, we allow it to consume us with fear, or worse, anger. The setbacks we feel because of unknown reasons, or even God's timing, can make us feel unheard at that moment. To be cliché for a moment remember: it's a marathon not a sprint - it's a *long road.*

All of us would like to believe that God hears our prayer and jumps into action - and He does, just not as we expect. There is preparation needed to advance in ways our hearts want but our minds aren't ready to grasp. An understanding that makes us stronger for trials that could come in the future. Then, there's the prayer God doesn't answer because it's not what's best for us at all. Hard part is it takes a long time to see it.

Your faith journey is a long road - a lifelong race with many events to discern with future revelations that connect the dots. Don't be derailed by thinking God isn't working fast enough, or He has forgotten about you. Throughout it all, continue to offer up prayers in order to be rescued, but surrender them for God to handle. The courage to trust God with it all helps you see the beauty that He knows you better than anyone.

*Think about your life in reverse - see where God's timing was perfect, or His way ended up being much better.*

# JOURNAL

# God Incidences

*"Then they asked each other, 'Were not our hearts burning within us while he talked with us on the road and opened the Scriptures to us?'" (Lk 24:32)*

Recognizing Christ in our lives daily is part of the beauty of our faith. These are times when coincidences become "God incidences" because we're open to enjoy our encounter with the living God.

If we're suffering from tunnel vision as a result of being too caught up in life, we'll could miss the answer to our prayers or times we're called to help others.

Think about the disciples who traveled on the road to Emmaus (Lk 24:1-32) focusing on themselves and their own problems, not realizing Jesus was alongside them. They're so lost in the hurt that even when Christ shows up, they have no idea it's Him. Then, Jesus breaks the bread which they would have seen as the reminder of their relationship with Him - at that moment their eyes opened to see He was there the whole journey.

The Lord is always revealing himself in wondrous ways. We simply need to look beyond ourselves to notice He is there. Remain open to the times you would normally categorize as *strange coincidences*, and instead trust your faith - listen to the Father, be guided by the Holy Spirit and allow yourself to see Christ opening your eyes to something profound.

*Identify the times in your day that you can look back and see it was God's hand and not just a coincidence...*

# JOURNAL

# Time to Reset

*"We must pay the careful attention to what we have heard, so that we do not drift away." (Heb 2:1)*

God's been resetting humanity since the original sin of Adam and Eve. We read about it through all the covenants in the Old Testament until we finally receive the gift of Jesus Christ as the New Covenant. There were people who started out on the right track and lost their way: Noah, Abraham, Moses, and David.

Unfortunately, God finds it necessary to have to start all over again when people stray away from living their faith. This isn't just something that takes place in the Bible. While we don't control the ways of how our entire society behaves, we do have to make ourselves more accountable.

You must discern what you've placed above God - things you worship more than the Creator. One way to re-order your devotion and relationship is to hit reset by offering personal sacrifices that prove your faithfulness. If we don't do it ourselves, just like Scripture, God will eventually shake things up to get our attention.

If you make the effort daily to think about what is leading you away from God, returning to back to Him won't be that far away. Reset and renew your bond with the Father, proving you want to spend eternity in His Kingdom by reconnecting with Him in every way.

*Thoroughly examine your life at this moment and see the areas you need to reset to put God first.*

# JOURNAL

# RIGHT JUDGEMENT

*"I will instruct you and teach you the way you should go; I will counsel you..." (Psalm 32:8)*

This gift of RIGHT JUDGEMENT is also known as "*Counsel.*" In other words, it really is the advice of the Holy Spirit, our moral common sense, we seek when having to make decisions which we hope are good choices. Simply said, it is choosing between right and wrong.

Acting on impulse can have some pretty rough consequences. We have to pause for a moment to think about how a choice we make or something we do either leads us closer to God or further away from Him. It's not about settling for pleasure in the moment but doing what is good for our final end to spend eternity with the God who loves us.

All your decisions must be about doing what is right for your family, friends, and humanity, not just what's best for you. To look at it another way, don't just think about how God thinks of you, but instead, what does the devil think of your choices?

In the end, the ultimate question I always tell people to ask when faced with tough choices is "God, what should I do?" It is then that we bring the Spirit in our decisions so we might be infused with the gift of RIGHT JUDGEMENT to assist our own free will.

*Are there decisions you're faced with or making that you need Right Judgement to ask, "God what should I do?"*

# JOURNAL

# Managing Expectations

*"All of you, be like-minded, be sympathetic, love one another, be compassionate and humble." (1Pt 3:8)*

Whether it's a family get together, a church potluck, or a work function, things don't always turn out as we want. It can be defeating when gatherings fall short of what we had hoped for or expected.

Different beliefs offer another dimension to gathering. Especially when it's people close to us, we might find ourselves struggling with those who are not in the same place with their faith life as we are. We all grow and change at different rates. Our dreams, experiences, and how they affect us can make us feel like the oddball out whether we feel it's *them* or *us*.

However, we must take advantage of this time and work to meet loved ones where they are on their journey. In times of disappointment or frustration, we must turn to prayer to manage our expectations. We must not place an unrealistic expectation on them with images of the person we want them to be. After all, when we read Scripture or offer our own prayers, don't we desire for God to meet us where we are?

Be who God created you to be and work to faithfully manage your expectations. It just might be your mercy, compassion or living example which brings a loved one back to God or the church.

*How can you set your expectations to meet the needs of those who love you? Commit to righting any wrongs.*

# JOURNAL

# Acts of Charity

*"Each of you should use whatever gift you have received to serve others, as faithful stewards of God's grace in its various forms." (1Pt 4:10)*

The heart of what we do and why we do it is as important as the act itself. While working to lessen the burdens of others, it's not always about doing acts of charity we're comfortable with but remaining obedient to God's specific call for us in order to fulfill His plan. Nor can we just look back and say, "Look at all the wonderful things I do for others!" God just might reply with, "Yes, but is this what I asked of you?"

Charitable thinking allows us to see the fullness in what we are doing to help. It might be easy to write a check for a donation. For others, it could be serving in a ministry that they lost joy in and only show up to go through the motions. In our attempts to be Christ like, we must aspire to encounter others and offer the same type of charity Jesus did in the manner he offered healing. Christ simply didn't cure the blind but changed their soul by reading their heart.

Recognize that in caring for the less fortunate, it's not about the type of deed you do, but rather how deeply you're giving of yourself completely. Even if it stretches your comfort level. In all *acts of charity*, it's God's grace that flows out from us and not merely our own desires to feel good about doing good.

*How can you serve your community in a new way or stretch yourself to change the way you're involved now?*

# JOURNAL

# Who Do You Say I Am?

*"The one who says he abides in Him ought himself to walk in the same manner as He walked." (1Jn 2:6)*

"*Who Do You Say I Am*? (Mt 16:15) is one of the most pivotal questions defining our faith. It's about so much more than the titles the Apostles recite back to Jesus when asked this question. Today, Christ is still asking us this question as we work to be in relationship with Him. Do we really ponder who He truly is?

We're asked to answer this question by looking inward, not outward. You show the world who He is by how you are living your life as a believer. Authentic men and women of Christ know that the answer to who Jesus is relies on everything that we do and say as representatives of His mission. To know Jesus Christ, is to experience Jesus Christ.

Jesus did not want the answer in words then, and He doesn't want it that way now. He desires keepers of the Kingdom. Disciples who are willing to proclaim truth in love and lead the people around them to the Father in Heaven just as He did. He needs us to be His church through the truth of the Gospel in our own actions. So, if like Peter our answer is faithfully given as, "*You are Lord and Messiah*" then accepting Christ, means we "take on" all of who He is, was, and always will be. His persecution, His works, and His love for others so people can experience who He is forever through us.

*What's your answer in words when Jesus asks, "Who do you say I am?" Can you be better at living the answer?*

# JOURNAL

# Share Your Story

*"Your light must shine before others, that they see your good deeds and glorify your heavenly Father." (Mt 5:16)*

Our church wouldn't have grown had the disciples stayed in the upper room, or Paul's testimony been left in some journal. Neither would people share in the incredible grace the Saints experienced through their works if their holiness only focused on personal prayer. All who share their testimony, spread the message of the power in a life shared with Jesus Christ.

The bible isn't just history, the people aren't just characters. Just like the power of Scripture, sharing our story plays the same part for our generation. We're called to let others know how Christ is present in our lives. We must be willing to tell *"anyone with ears to hear"* (Mk 4:23) of the goodness we find through our faith. Otherwise, how will they know of God's grace?

In addition to Scripture and church Tradition, most people need to hear everyday examples of real people living faith. Our backstories validate us. Common life experiences help connect us and open doors for a greater spiritual bond. Our story is possibly the final piece needed for another person to find the strength to surrender themselves. Whether the witness you share is based on triumph, never-ending hope, or simply the spirit-filled peace you strive to have, there is someone in this world who needs to hear you share your story.

*Regardless of where you are on your faith journey, what story do you have to share that can inspire others?*

# JOURNAL

# Make the Effort

*"I have fought the good fight. I have completed the race. I have kept the faith." (2Tm 2:15)*

We should always be putting our best foot forward to help others see the beauty of faith. God sees the effort we give Him whether we fall short of our goals or whether we convert many hearts living our faith. He's asking us to make an attempt with the gifts we're given.

Maybe you think you're not equipped with the right gifts or you aren't at a certain level of holiness to do what God is asking. That's not the way it works - we are called to give our best and let God handle the rest.

One of the best examples of lack of effort is Jonah. He was unwilling to go to Nineveh because it was going to be hard work. He wasn't even open to make the effort to save the people where God was sending Him. Eventually God gets His way after Jonah spends three days in the belly of a whale. What's the moral of the story? Make the effort our Lord desires or you might just be eaten by a whale... and nobody wants that.

Never forget the world around us is trying to snatch our attention and focus from what the Father wants from us. It is so important we shed the selfish behaviors which do not allow us to fully conform to who God created us to be and rob us of making an effort to build His kingdom on Earth.

*What situation has God been calling you into that you have delayed in answering Him? What's your next step?*

# JOURNAL

# Back to the Basics

*"We do not know what we ought to pray for, but the Spirit himself intercedes for us..." (Rom 8:26)*

Imagine if you never grew, never learned anything, never advanced through life experiences. Truth is, nothing ever stays the same. Problem is, as we get older, we forget the beauty of what life was like as a child or even what it was like when we started our favorite hobby or sport.

Ironically the same thing happens in our relationship with Jesus. Our faith, prayer life, and even how we see the world transform gets clouded. While our faith opens us up to the beauty of everything our Lord offers us, and it's all positive, if we're not careful then we can overcomplicate it. We can feel ourselves lost or overwhelmed as habits and experiences change.

In these moments we need to get back to the basics. We must settle into church teachings, its models of prayer, the inspiration of the Saints, and quiet time to listen that give us the chance to slow down to simply be present with God.

Yes, our personal encounters with Christ change over time, but the foundation of who we are as Christians can always bring us back to where we long to be. For all of us, there comes a time when we need to stop trying so hard and just get back to the basics.

*What would you consider some basics of faith? How can you get back to the ones you have over complicated?*

# JOURNAL

# KNOWLEDGE

*"An intelligent heart acquires knowledge, and the ear of the wise seeks knowledge. (Prov 18:15)*

KNOWLEDGE perfects the virtue of faith. This gift helps us understand where we made mistakes in our day, and what we need to do in order to make our wrongs right. Each time we examine our conscience or prepare for Reconciliation, it's important to call on the Holy Spirit to assist us with the gift of KNOWLEDGE.

Think about a recent argument with someone. Our passion and pride convince us we're right and if something doesn't end well, we're the victim. We know that's not always the case and sometimes we are the instigator, or our demeanor is "less than inviting."

We use KNOWLEDGE to discern the *how*, the *why*, and the *what* which could have caused us to be less than who we desire to be for God. It could also be said that we are seeing ourselves *through* the eyes of God. While we aren't in need of more guilt when we fall short, we need to know what we have to work on.

When it comes to our own decision making, this gift of the Spirit evaluates ways that we've grown closer to God or been separated from His grace through sin. KNOWLEDGE helps us to confidently distinguish God's voice from the whispers the Devil uses to tempt us. This gift is the key to refocus who God has created us to be.

*Pray each day for the enlightenment of Knowledge. Call on the Holy Spirit and fully examine your daily actions.*

# JOURNAL

# Self-Image

*"The Father has loved us so much that we are called children of God. And we really are his children." (1Jn 3:1)*

The greatest critic any of us can have is the person staring back at us in the mirror. If we think negatively of ourselves, the flaws we see are very real even if they only exist in our minds. The reverse is also dangerous if ego and self-righteousness take over, causing us to miss things that could use a little work. Insecurity stems from thinking little of yourself, while arrogance blossoms from a blind view that you don't possess any flaws.

Becoming exactly who God created us to be is filled with a few obstacles; ranging from doubt, to inadequacies we're ashamed of, mental illness, or even just times we feel that we've let God down. This level of thinking persuades us that we're unworthy of a relationship with God. Truth is, because you are a Child of God you are *always* worthy.

Throughout your life, you will question if you can truly do all it takes to allow yourself to be consumed by the love of Christ. Alternatively, there will also be moments that despite your trials, you see the brilliance of God's unending love at work – soak it in. We have a God who takes us with our battle scars, fears, failures, and all the parts that aren't so pretty. No matter what side your self-image sits on, just know, we don't have to be perfect for Christ's love, just willing to accept it.

*Take an honest inventory of your current self-image. Do you need to change it? How do you see God in you?*

# JOURNAL

# Enjoying Creation

*"For in him all things were created: things in heaven and on earth, visible and invisible…" (Col 1:16)*

I once heard a priest offer a reminder of the beauty God gives us to experience in the world. He said, "I believe that when we go to heaven God will ask us this question: 'Did you enjoy my creation?'" This is deeply touching and a recognition that all of us need to pay more attention to - we all need to enjoy His creation.

How often do we stand in awe and marvel at the beautiful world He gave us? The way the sun rises, or the stars light up the night sky when we stop long enough to take notice. And sometimes when letting the dog out at 3:00 AM, it's all we have to make us smile.

From unique animals to breathtaking landscapes to basic food for nourishment, and even the beauty of the sound of a laughing baby, everything we see, and experience comes from the hand of God.

In an age of electronics and busy schedules, we have the tendency to miss the world around us. We've almost forgotten what it's like to stare out a window on a car ride. It is now a conscious effort to take the time to look up and take in your surroundings.

Let's take notice to be in awe of all God has made. Enjoying creation is part of our faith. God entrusted everything to us so we wouldn't live apart from His love.

*This week, when travelling anywhere in a car or on a walk, do not use electronics. What do you notice?*

# JOURNAL

# I Need You

*"Let each of you look not only to his own interests, but also to the interests of others." (Phil 2:4)*

"I need you." These quite possibly could be the three hardest words we utter in our life. Three strong, powerful, beautiful words making a declaration that we can't do everything alone.

Still, we tend to view this statement as a sign of weakness and not strength. It's as though we have become so convinced, we have to do everything on our own for our own glory that we've forgotten the bond we have with others. God places specific people in our lives to help us joyfully fulfill our purpose - loved ones who complete us.

This is also a key phrase in surrendering to the Lord. It takes all the courage in the world to finally get to a point where we trust Him enough, get on our knees, and say, "I need you." Whether it's a crying out in distress or just a whisper to express what our heart feels, we are incomplete without telling God, our *Abba* (Father), our need.

Maybe it saves our marriage, a child-parent relationship, or even you. Be brave, tell those closest to you today that you need them but only after looking up to the Heavens peace and trust, offering your admittance to the One who made you, "*I need you*."

*Who must you tell in your life, "I need you?" Are there others you need to be closer or part of major decisions?*

# JOURNAL

# Severed Grace

*"...As the Scripture says, "God resists the proud, but gives grace to the humble." (James 4:6)*

God's grace – we're told it's what we need to get to Heaven and is our guiding force to "save" us in this life. What happens when we don't want it? By sinning or living a life outside of one pleasing to God, we're not allowing our self to receive what God gives us freely.

Imagine it like this... God's grace flows into our soul through a pipeline. Anything you choose over Him would be like you pushing it aside, severing us from the grace He's trying to pour into us. It doesn't matter the name we give it: pride, fear, greed, lust, attitude, envy, or jealousy, it all has the same effect.

We must look inward to identify the thing stalling us from growth in our faith. When we are spiritually burdened or empty, we must concentrate on the cause, not only the symptom. We can't ask God to fix what isn't broken on His end. When the pipeline is severed, you have to put it back together and let it fill you again.

Identify what has severed your "grace line" then prayerfully reflect on the best way to repair it. Look past your own struggles to once again feel refreshed in a shower of the only thing that can make you alive. God's grace stream continues to flow, no matter what, you must choose to accept it.

*What habits or feelings are not allowing you fully accept the grace God is pouring out to you?*

# JOURNAL

# HOPE

*"Hope does not put us to shame, because God's love has been poured out into our hearts through the Holy Spirit, who has been given to us." (Rom 5:5)*

HOPE can be a rough word to think about when we don't want to wait for a situation to change that's weighing on us. We must realize though, our desire for HOPE is fulfilled by inspiring triumphs that come out of situations when all seems lost. The resurrection of Jesus Christ certainly offers us all the HOPE we could desire.

Through it we begin to understand that HOPE isn't merely something created by our own inner thinking. Instead, it's something offered through our actions to trust in God as we move forward despite anything that is going on at the current moment. If we struggle to find HOPE, we must give it a chance to spring forth by being the image of Christ to the world around us.

HOPE stands for: ***H**elping **O**thers **P**repare **E**very day.* By taking the focus of ourselves, we begin to understand that we find our own HOPE by supporting others to find theirs. In sacrificing for those in greater need than us, we're transformed to see how our living example is what God is using in order to save others.

Live out God's desires even when you struggle to understand them. In the HOPE you share to heal others you'll see God is already working to give you HOPE too.

*What ways can you find HOPE by helping others? Make a "go-to" list of outreach to do when you feel hopeless.*

# JOURNAL

# What's God Asking?

*"Before I formed you in the womb I knew you, before you were born I set you apart…" (Jer 1:5)*

We are called to reflect on the following question daily: *"What's God asking of me?"* When we reflect on how God is trying to use us, it prevents us from becoming complacent. It challenges us to see ourselves as an available instrument at any point. The initial answer may not come in words, but instead by someone who is placed on our path.

Spending time in prayer to hear God's desires for us can make all the difference in understanding three things: why we are where we are at this moment, how to prepare for what God wants, and what to do next.

Imagine if Mary and Joseph failed to be open to continuously asking, *"God what are you asking of me?"* So much of their journey and faith-filled decisions would have been clouded by angst and confusion. By allowing this question to be their beacon in the night, they both were open to follow God's plan to bring Christ into the world by trusting the Holy Spirit.

God's answers are not going to always leave you feeling comfortable. One thing we all know, He always has our best interest in mind, so you can't go wrong by following the only One who can fulfill us. Despite numerous twists and turns, just like the Holy Family, you can rest assured you are never left alone.

*Start each day inquiring, "God what are you asking of me?" Prayerfully listen for His answer. Write it down.*

# JOURNAL

# COURAGE

*"... Be strong and courageous. Do not be afraid; do not be discouraged, for the Lord your God will be with you wherever you go." (Josh 1:9)*

Boldly living our faith out loud can be one of the most difficult aspects of being a Christian. The gift of COURAGE gives us the ability to do things we never thought we could do when it comes to our faith.

Also known as *"Fortitude,"* COURAGE goes far beyond enlightening our mind or simply opening our eyes. It reinforces our will to push forward, actively living what we believe when there's a need. This gift is described as the one that gives "strength to the soul."

By relying on COURAGE, we become strong to do our part to seize the moment to make the world a better place. It helps us pass on God's word to our friends, family and all those we normally might not share our faith with. Possibly, next time you're in public and you see someone in distress, you'll have what you need to say, "How are you?," share a prayer or offer encouragement in a way you never would before.

Even in our own lives, COURAGE assists us to overcome our fears to live a Christian lifestyle to place God above all other things; even if the world might be trying to tell us they are more important. Trust God and be COURAGEOUS to do what was once impossible.

*Don't hold back, commit to one act of faith-filled courage today. Write about it and who it was for.*

# JOURNAL

# Comfortably Numb

---

*"Wake up, strengthen what remains and is about to die, I have not found your works complete." (Rev 3:2)*

---

Getting caught up in the "routines" of our "church" faith, or other religious traditions, can sometimes be a trap within our personal faith life. We can find ourselves taking things for granted by allowing Mass, Sacraments, or personal prayers to lose their luster as just another item on the checklist. Nothing in our relationship with God should be allowed to get stale, or we risk becoming disconnected from the entire Trinity.

This spiritual laziness is something I refer to as "Comfortably Numb." Quite frankly, this is part of the reason people can struggle with organized religion. If we fall victim and become numb to what we experience through Christ, we stop feeling God's real presence and it prevents our hearts from encountering Him. When this happens, we simply go through the motions of what the church offers because that's what we are "supposed" to do as an attendee or member – we leave our faith life up to someone else. To be fair, this spiritual phenomenon strikes Christians regardless of where they worship if they are not careful.

You are invited to change up your comfortable practices, to discover a more fulfilling relationship with The Father, The Son, and the Holy Spirit.

---

*Find a new way you can challenge yourself to grow in your relationship with Christ. New prayer routines, extra worship/Mass, or an awareness of Christ in the world.*

---

# JOURNAL

# Ultimate Respect

*"A new commandment I give to you, that you love one another, even as I have loved you, that you also love one another. By this all men will know you are My disciples, if you have love for one another." (Jn 13:34-35)*

A friend of mine once said we should take every place the word "love" appears in the bible and replace it with the phrase, "ultimate respect." Taking it one step further, I would say we should do the same in our own life. The truest meaning of love cannot be shared without having the utmost respect for the other person.

Without respect, even the most emotional of feelings will often turn into selfish relationships where we make it all about us. The absence of ultimate respect between two people leaves a void where there aren't intentions to say, "I'm sorry" or "I want what is best for you" and certainly not, "I live for you."

Need a model of ultimate respect? Think of Jesus. Jesus Christ's love story with us endured all the events that led Him up to and on the cross. Everything He went through was to show us how much He believes in us by offering Himself with this type of love.

We must continue to live a life that all our actions, relationships, and daily encounters are carried out in the image of Christ - with love, kind words, and intentional efforts based on ultimate respect for others.

*How are you showing respect for to your family or who you're in a relationship with? Can you be better?*

# JOURNAL

# Setbacks

---

*"I can do all things through Christ who strengthens me." (Phil 4:13)*

---

Starting over with new routines or trying to get back to old ones can be hard to jump start. Especially if we are trying to work towards our goals without acknowledging why we haven't kept up pursuing them. It is vital to name the setbacks we've had in the past, identify why they occurred, and think through the impact previous failures have had on us.

Our planning should contain how we will move forward when what set us back in the first place starts to creep in. Face it. if we don't deal with the setbacks that prevented us from accomplishment before, they will stunt the growth we're searching for now.

Despite the fact they delay the date of our goals, setbacks can be the best thing to happen to us. They show us that even though we've fallen, we still get through it. They drive us to be better. Setbacks can be the blessing that hit us so hard, our ego and pride flee leaving us to find humility. We all have setbacks.

As you prepare your next workout plan, dream of a business milestone, or surrender to your goal for a closer relationship with God, confront your past setbacks. Just your willingness to make the effort means you can do this because the mind is a powerful asset!

---

*List what prevents you from accomplishing your goals... make a plan to finish whatever you're starting.*

---

# JOURNAL

# Recognizing Jesus

*"...Jesus put his hands on the man's eyes. Then his eyes were opened, his sight was restored..." (Mk 8:25)*

If Jesus was before you in this moment, would you recognize Him? Throughout our day despite how much effort we put in to finding God daily, we can look back at the end of the day and realize how many times we missed Him when He was present.

The Pharisees who claimed to be the holiest of people and in touch with God more than anyone could not recognize Jesus as the Son of God. Their own pride blinded them of what and who they were waiting to see. What else could He have shown them? They were never going to be happy because it was all about what they thought they wanted instead of being focused on God before them. The Holy Trinity (the *Father*, the *Son*, and the *Holy Spirit*) aren't confined to one single human presence we see and proclaim, "Oh that's them!"

To recognize Jesus, we must be ready. Today, He will be in the child's eyes that look at you with every ounce of love. He's an elderly person crossing the parking lot who tests your patience. He might be the police officer who writes you a ticket for speeding because God needed to protect you from the harm ahead. Let go of what you "think" He looks like to see His signs are everywhere. We just need to choose to recognize Him always and in unlikely places.

*Be intentional about seeing Jesus in your day. Where was He? How was He present? Did you miss Him at all?*

# JOURNAL

# Persecution

*"Blessed are those persecuted for the sake of righteousness, the kingdom of heaven is theirs" (Mt 5:10)*

When you commit to living a life of faith, there will be haters. People who want to tear you down or even harm you for loving Jesus. Maybe you've experienced this and can easily agree. If you're just beginning your faith walk this can be hard to understand. How is it that trying to live a life dedicated to service and holy inspiration can make others angry?

We're all being tested in some way for what we believe; no one is immune. It comes in many forms from different people – it isn't always the radical lashing out portrayed on the nightly news. Persecution comes in the form of the denial of who you are as a believer. Maybe even more sadly, persecution doesn't always come from the outside, it can come from those we love or even people in our own church. Are you willing to stand up for what you believe, or does it make you slowly retreat into silence?

A review of history shows us this has been happening since the beginning of time. We must remain strong enough to be brave for Christ but mindful to respond in love rather than with the same evil or hate projected to hurt us. Never think it will be any different for us then it was for the One who died on the cross under persecution for proclaiming truth and love.

*Is there a time you've been surprised by others negative reactions toward your faith? How did you feel or react?*

# JOURNAL

# Responsibility

*"From everyone who has been given much, much will be required." (Lk 12:48)*

The word responsibility literally means that we are "able to respond." If we have air in our lungs and God gives us the gift of today, it's our responsibility to face anything in front of us - bad or good.

There are periods of time we have a responsibility to carry our own cross with burdens. Then there are stretches where we are blessed with abundance. There can be an even bigger responsibility during times of abundance to manage what we have been given. Falling into the trap of gluttony, or coveting as much as we can, leads us straight into sin and must be avoided at all cost.

We also have the responsibility of those entrusted in our care to lead them in the right direction. This could mean not just walking past someone in need or looking the other way to avoid an interaction.

Responsibility is a big word. Wherever you are in life, whatever you have in this moment, handle it responsibly. Whether material things, life situations, or people, don't ask why you have to handle the things you do, instead see them as a sign of grace that God believes in you. As the line from the movie *Spiderman* puts it, "With great power comes great responsibility."

*Where do you shy away from the responsibility you have to take care of things/people at home, work, or school?*

# JOURNAL

# REVERENCE

*"He is your praise and He is your God, who has done these great and awesome things for you which your eyes have seen." (Dt 10:21)*

The second to last gift of the Holy Spirit relates to the *joyful* awareness of our faith. It is about offering the respect to God that He deserves as an act of love. REVERENCE, or *"Piety"* as it is also known, allows us to celebrate seeing Christ in our midst opening us up to what they truly are supposed to be through encountering the divine. It's the key to transformation.

Looking around our churches, by the demeanor on some faces, it could be said we don't pray for this gift enough and we need to call on reverence a little more. Maybe we think because we show up, God shows up and that should be enough. Still, our joyful REVERENCE is needed in order to inspire others to crave a dynamic relationship with God to better their own lives.

Allow holy moments to be truly "holy" by calling on the Spirit to enlighten you. As Pope Francis tells us, *"Reverence is synonymous for friendship with God; that friendship into which Jesus introduces us, and that changes our lives and fills our soul with joy and peace."*

Allow REVERENCE to take over the way you do all things in your faith to show others you are lifted up by the beauty of the promises of our Lord.

*While praying for REVERENCE, how can you do a better job allowing others to see your respect for Jesus?*

# JOURNAL

# Striving for Perfection

---

*"Not that I have already obtained it or have already become perfect, but I press on..." (Phil 3:12)*

---

In life, we tend to get caught up in details. We want everything to be perfectly ordered. However, we know this isn't the way things eventually fall into place. It's important to know that this also happens even in the manner we live to grow in faith.

The fantasy vision of faith projects every prayer moment in a serene, quiet setting. It makes us think a Christ-like apology always mends every relationship instantly. "Perfect faith" would have us experiencing God in a way that leaves us floating out of church each Mass or worship service. It might even make us think that everyone we share our faith with will receive us with open arms and can't wait to hear more. The truth is, perfect faith is found in the mess of life, believing even when we want to give up.

The beauty of our journey though is *striving for perfection*. Trying, working, and fully living out our purpose even when the results are less than expected. Trusting that the seeds we plant will be perfect in their own way, in God's time, for His plan.

So, do we hope to be perfect? *Yes*. But in faith, we can't become so focused on it that when we fall short, we give up all together or feel unworthy. Keep striving!

---

*What do you focus on that has to be "perfect?" How can you put them into the perspective of this reflection?*

---

# JOURNAL

# Abba

*"Because you are sons, God sent forth the Spirit of His Son into our hearts, crying, "Abba, Father!" (Gal 4:6)*

I believe there are certain words we use that call us into a deeper level of spirituality. One of those words is the name Jesus utters for His father in Heaven: *"Abba."* We might say the word "God" all the time, or pray "Our Father," but to use the same language as Christ offers us a unique connection with Him.

*Abba* is Aramaic for "Father." To use this specific term when we pray, is an imitation of the Son who shows ultimate respect for His Father. For us, it's a deeper reminder that we are forever a child of God, no matter what we've done or where we've been.

If you're a parent, you know there is nothing you wouldn't do for your child. As a child, you also know that if your parents are involved in your life, there isn't anything they would make you face alone.

In our faith, Jesus' use of the word *Abba* puts on display His obedience. Everything He did was about leading people to His Father and not about Himself. Christ desired salvation for all so they could return to God and live eternity in His presence. Christ wants the same for us.

Today, before your day ends, get on your knees and say the words "Abba, thank you for loving me."

*Are there any words in the bible or religious education you don't understand? Look up a new word each day.*

# JOURNAL

# Seasons of Life

*"For everything there is a season, and a time for every matter under heaven." (Ecc 3:1)*

Maybe you've heard the term "*seasons of life*." This relates to friendships, careers, community, and even prayer life. We all experience times where the seasons of life mirror nature regardless of what time of year it is. Our personal "winters" of despair can hit mid-summer whether we want them to or not.

One example is people who come into our lives for only a short time to help us learn a lesson or experience what God wants and then move on for one reason or another. It can hurt deeply if we're not ready, especially if we invest all our self into relationships.

Even the disciples had to experience this after Jesus' resurrection - forty days later He leaves again, ascending to Heaven. Still, Christ kept His promise to bring about a new season by sending the Holy Spirit.

The hardest thing in the world can be letting go of something or someone we hold dear. In these times our faith is tested, and our trust must be placed in accepting God's grace as we move forward.

Mindful of the Spirit, may we accept that growth comes from change. Allow the seasons of life to offer preparation, hope, joy, and closure.

*Identify some recent change of seasons. Pray for thanksgiving and strength to let go of what was meant to only prepare you to receive greater things ahead.*

# JOURNAL

# Why So Serious?

*"For you have been told, what is good, and what the Lord requires of you: Only to do justice and to love goodness, and to walk humbly with your God."* (Mic 6:8)

Some of us fall victim to thinking "our way" is the best way - or the only way. However, we need to remain open to see things in a different manner. We can take ourselves so seriously that we forget to see the value in other people's ideas or insights. With this level of thinking, we are only willing to experience things the way we normally do.

Our willingness to recognize the Lord in fresh ways is important too. Life is ever changing, and our faith is ever growing. Just because you had an amazing encounter one way or with a certain prayer doesn't mean you always will, nor does it mean that is the only way other people can have the same walk with Christ. We must remove the habit of only doing things the way we like and adapt to styles related to the situation.

Filling our hearts with the joy is about remaining open to different methods or prayer styles that keep our relationship with God renewed. Don't take yourself so seriously. If you're falling victim to the same routines and only doing certain things you've always done, then seek out opportunities to go with the grace-filled flow where God wants to lead you. Encounter Him in ways like never before - even if it's somebody else's ideas.

*What have you been stuck doing "your way" or struggle to see as someone else does? How can you change?*

# JOURNAL

# Reflect

*"Do not conform to the pattern of this world, but be transformed by the renewing of your mind." (Rom 12:2)*

Technology has modified our attention span, how we process information, and how we communicate. Instantaneous internet searches and social media posts have all of us gravitating to small snippets of audio or text, so we get what we're looking for and move on. Even our churches are trying to teach us through modified methods to fit into a 140-character world.

As humans, we aren't able to process all the information we receive as quickly as we receive it. Sadly, we've stopped pausing to reflect on what we read and hear. We see it, give it a "like" and then move on to the next thing forgetting what we read five posts before. Yes, this is the age we live in, but it doesn't mean it has to rob us of the time we need to reflect and let something marinate within us. It's our choice.

Next time you see that inspirational saying or hear a Scripture verse that touches you, apply it to your current life situation and think about what it means to you. If it's meant for someone else, take the time to write a note and tell them why you are sharing.

Make the effort to stop and reflect more often. You'll see a stronger prayer life, conversations will be more fruitful, and life experiences will offer clarity.

*Take time to pray and reflect daily with the messages that impact your life. How can they help you grow?*

# JOURNAL

# Walking on Water

*"But when he saw the wind, he was afraid and, beginning to sink, cried out, "Lord, save me!" (Mt 14:30)*

Having faith while everything in life is great – smooth sailing is easy. But, it's how we're able to still praise God in the storm that identifies how deeply we believe. A struggle even the disciples who walked with Jesus shared.

Think of the Gospel story of Peter walking on the water in the storm (Mt 14:22-33). At first, he trusts and steps out among the giant waves. Even though he is doing it, doubt creeps in that he can stay on top of the waves. Peter stops looking at Jesus and fear causes him to begin to sink. Now, we have to remember that this story in Scripture comes immediately after Christ's miracle of *The Feeding the 5,000.* Peter saw all the miracles of Jesus – so there should be no doubt.

This story reminds us that that no matter how much God reveals His goodness and power, we can fall apart quickly when things get rough. When the waves of life are crashing all around, we must be brave enough to focus intently on Jesus one step at a time. If doubt creeps in, sincerely cry out, knowing Christ will be there with a strong hand to pull you up just like Peter

A life completely focused on Christ helps us do the seemingly impossible - even if its walking on water.

*Find a picture of Jesus or a religious item to help your human senses focus on Him while you pray today.*

# JOURNAL

# WONDER & AWE

*"Amazement seized them all, and they glorified God and were filled with awe, saying, 'We have seen extraordinary things today.'"* (Lk 5:26)

"*Fear of the Lord*" is an often-misunderstood gift of the Holy Spirit. Many of us hear the first word and are not aware of the beauty within. Even growing up, I always thought, "Why should we be afraid of God?" That isn't what it means though. "Fear" is really about our hope to never be separated by the love of God.

When we look at this gift by its other name, WONDER & AWE, it gives us the openness to recognize God in new ways. Not wanting to ever know a day without him by your side. A chance to actively look around you and remain aware of His presence in all of creation and feel His love in those close to you.

Psalm 111:10 says, "The fear of the LORD is the beginning of WISDOM." This shows us how all seven gifts of the Holy Spirit work in order to come full circle.

In the beginning of creation, Adam and Eve, lost site of the WONDER & AWE in the Garden. They denied themselves to see all God gave them, choosing sin to come between them and the one who created them. Let us pray to not suffer the same fate for one single moment. Allow WONDER & AWE to be your strong hold to never take God's love and majesty for granted.

*Find one aspect of creation to focus on. Be in awe of God's detail and thank Him this day as you reflect.*

# JOURNAL

# One More Thing

*"Whatever you have learned or received or heard from me, or seen in me—put it into practice. And the God of peace will be with you." (Phil 4:9)*

There's always *one more thing* that we can add to our day. One more task to complete on the checklist. The devil has committed to take our attention away from love and goodness by getting us to focus on the busyness of life. "*Busy*" has even become an answer to the question, "How are you?" That response doesn't tell people "how" we are, it tells them "what" we are. One of the biggest traps of free will we all can fall victim to is thinking there's always one more thing we need to be doing, instead of focusing on those we love most.

Yes, our work is important, especially if we feel we are doing it to be the image of Christ for other people. Work needs to be finished, chores need to get done and errands won't run themselves. However, we must never be too busy to take time for those closest to us.

I often remind people that the greatest "mission trip" we might ever take is to share faith and time with the people in our homes to feed the souls of those who crave our attention. Christ's work isn't always accomplished in another country, it is also done by answering the vocation we're called into with family. Yes, there will always be one more thing, but a healthy faith life begins by taking care of those you appreciate.

*What are the ways you can make sure you are saving time for loved ones amidst a busy lifestyle?*

# JOURNAL

# Taking Chances

*"Trust in the Lord with all your heart, and do not lean on your own understanding." (Prov 3:5)*

When someone says they are going to take some chances without fully knowing what the outcome will be or having a full-proof backup plan it is often called reckless. People see taking chances with a negative lens and categorize them as risky - even irresponsible. But it's how we take those chances and whether they are rooted in in our faith that changes everything.

God calls us to jump into the deep end every so often. Scripture is full of people who did something amazing when they took chances for the Lord.

- *Moses* looked to move forward when people wanted to go back to what was enslaving them
- *Twelve young men* left the world they knew to follow the One who would save the world.
- *Paul* stopped persecuting those he didn't understand and accepted a life in Christ.

Taking chances for God can be uncomfortable because it doesn't always conform with the world. You might not understand it. To make sure it is truly of Him, we must retreat, listen, encounter the Sacraments, and trust God to fully discern what is right. Remember, what you do today, can change a lot of tomorrows.

*Is there anything you have always thought of that would be too risky, but your heart still yearns to do it?*

# JOURNAL

# Thy Will Be Done

*"Thy kingdom come, thy will be done, on earth as it is in heaven." (Mt 6:10)*

Four powerful words give us the outline and mindset of how to live our life as Christians – "Thy will be done." When we've grown to a full life in Christ, we simply allow Him to live through us. Just like Jesus, it is always about what the Father wants - total obedience.

It's a very difficult phrase to prayerfully offer up. Can you give up complete control to pray, "Lord, I want my loved one's illness to be healed, but it's okay if you see it differently and need to take them from this earth?" When we put it that way, we may want to side step our commitment to say "Thy will be done." These powerful words aren't a new declaration though. We willfully say this every time we pray the *Our Father*.

We must embrace this acknowledgment of our trust in God. This is our "yes" to a commitment that God will never do anything to hurt us or punish us. He provides everything we need to handle every situation before us, even if it doesn't make sense to us or others.

You have prepared yourself, now it's time to live your life *with* God, not just *for* God. You must accept He is God and you are not. When the seas of life are stormy - Thy Will be Done. When things are great - Thy will be done. With every breath - Thy Will be Done.

*What gifts of the Spirit can help you most to surrender to be able to say, "Thy will be done" currently?*

# JOURNAL

# Why the Bee?

Our ministry's BEE logo represents the simplest reminder to humbly "be who God created you to be."

In a world that demands so much of our time and attention, we get stuck continually reaching for the golden carrot. Social media and lives lived in public make us envious of what others have or jealous of their gifts. The bee reminds us to take a step back and recognize all we are blessed with and our talents.

When we say, or pray, the words "Lord, let me be…" we don't have to finish the rest of the sentence. God needs to fill in the blanks with His will for us. It is not a message to under achieve, but rather to excel by understanding what is within you already.

So today and every day, remember to pause and simply pray, "Let me be…"  then surrender to listen for God's response back.

**FOR**
**SPECIAL ACCESS,**
**ADDITIONAL VIDEOS,**
**& OTHER**
**AUDIO REFLECTIONS**
**GO TO:**

**www.FaithandRealLife.com/GotaMinute**

# About the Author

Greg Wasinski is an internationally recognized, Inspirational Speaker and Author from Cleveland, OH. He also offers his radio talents as a featured host on SiriusXM Radio's, *The Catholic Channel* and EWTN Radio. He is the voice and personality of multiple podcasts, the Faith 180 video series, and is recognized on social media for his faith-based motivation. Additional TV/Radio appearances include, EWTN, Catholic TV, Clear Channel, NBC, and ABC.

Greg is also the Founder and Executive Director of the non-profit corporation, LMBM Inc. The ministry is a missionary based organization serving as an extension of the church with content that is inspiring, relative, and quality church teaching. Our *"Faith and Real Life"* resources and presentations reach out to those who are disconnected from faith or are looking for a deeper understanding of "why they believe what they believe"

Prior to his life in ministry Greg had a career for thirteen years as a corporate executive in both the marketing and golf course industries. He continues to offer business coaching and motivational work sessions to companies who are serious about customer service, a team-based work environment, and servant leadership-based management.

Greg Wasinski holds a certificate in Catholic Scriptural Theology from John Paul the Great University. He is married to his wife Aimee and they are the parents of two children.

**www.GregWasinski.com**

# Contact Information

LMBM Inc.

8584 B East Washington St.

#108

Chagrin Falls, OH 44023

www.FaithandRealLife.com

admin@lmbminc.org

LMBM Inc. is a registered 501(c)3
non-profit corporation.

If you would like to support the missionary efforts of the ministry, please send donations to the address above or contributions are also accepted online at: **www.BeeADonor.com**

# Also Available:

***"Where Faith & Real Life Come Together..."*** is a faith-filled inspirational book with thirty-one short chapters to discover and recognize all the ways faith plays out in the world around us. This compilation of stories, coupled with reflection questions, will help you notice how God is at work every day. Perfect no matter where you are on your faith journey.

***"All I Ever Have to Be..."*** Audio CD is a combination of songs featuring the beautiful vocals of Aimee Wasinski, and the authentically genuine reflections of Inspirational Speaker and Author, Greg Wasinski. This CD helps remind you to be who God created you to be. An amazing collection to share with family, friends and members of your faith community.

**Products can also be ordered in bulk for a discounted price. Inquire for details. www.FaithandRealLife.com**

Made in the USA
Monee, IL
09 March 2020

22876556R00072